MW01031490

handing on the faith

Other ***Handing on the Faith*** titles:

When You Are a Confirmation Sponsor

When You Are a Godparent

Your Child's Baptism

Your Child's Confirmation

Your Child's First Communion

Your Child's First Penance

RCIA

_____

Candidate

_____

Sponsor

_____

Date

_____

Bishop or Priest

_____

Church

_____

Address

_____

City, State

When You Are an RCIA Sponsor

Rita Burns Senseman

ST. ANTHONY MESSENGER PRESS

Cincinnati, Ohio

Nihil Obstat
Rev. Hilarion Kistner, O.F.M.
Rev. Robert Hagedorn

Imprimi Potest
Rev. Fred Link, O.F.M.
Provincial

Imprimatur
+Most Rev. Carl K. Moeddel
Vicar General and Auxiliary Bishop
Archdiocese of Cincinnati
March 26, 2001

Scripture citations are taken from the *New Revised Standard Version Bible,* copyright ©1989 by the Division of Christian Education of the National Council of Churches of Christ in the U.S.A., and used by permission. All rights reserved.

Excerpts from the English translation of the *Catechism of the Catholic Church* for the United States of America, copyright ©1994 Libreria Editrice Vaticana—United States Catholic Conference, Inc. Used with permission. Excerpts from the English translation of the *Catechism of the Catholic Church: Modifications From the* Editio Typica, copyright ©1994 Libreria Editrice Vaticana—United States Catholic Conference, Inc.

Excerpts from the English translation of *Rite of Christian Initiation of Adults,* copyright ©1985, International Committee on English in the Liturgy, Inc. All rights reserved.

Cover and interior illustrations by Julie Lonneman
Cover and book design by Mary Alfieri

ISBN 0-86716-449-2

Published by St. Anthony Messenger Press
www.AmericanCatholic.org
Printed in the U.S.A.

Contents

Introduction

Congratulations! You have been chosen for a very important ministry—to be a sponsor for a person who wants to be a full member of the Roman Catholic Church. That is, you have been chosen to be a sponsor for a person participating in the Rite of Christian Initiation of Adults, commonly called "RCIA."

As a sponsor you will accompany a person who is on a journey of faith. You may accompany or sponsor someone who is seeking Baptism. Or, you may sponsor someone who is already baptized in another Christian tradition. Or, you may sponsor someone who is a baptized Catholic, but had no further formation in the Catholic faith. In any case, each person's journey is unique and filled with many wondrous stories. You will probably feel honored to accompany a person who is on a journey toward a deeper relationship with our loving God. The culmination of this journey of initiation is the celebration of the Sacraments of Initiation: Baptism, Confirmation and Eucharist, or Confirmation and Eucharist for those already baptized.

Thank you for saying yes to your call to be a sponsor. Many people find that serving in this role renews and enriches their own faith. It is also a great help to your parish. Your time and service are greatly appreciated. Your parish will support and help you in this ministry.

This booklet will help you better understand the role and specific responsibilities of the sponsor. First, we'll describe the process of initiation as envisioned by the *Rite of Christian Initiation of Adults* (hereafter known as "the Rite"). Second, we'll describe the role of the sponsor as it is given to us in the Rite. Third, we'll give you some very practical and helpful hints for being a good sponsor. Throughout the book you will find reflection questions for you to consider or discuss with a group of parish sponsors.

Also, you will find references to help you ground your ministry in the tradition of the Church: a quotation from the Church's liturgical book on initiation, the *Rite of Christian Initiation of Adults*; a quotation from the Bible; and a quotation from the *Catechism of the Catholic Church* or another Church document.

Please note that a person who is in the process of initiation can be called an inquirer, catechumen, candidate or elect. The differences will be described later. To make things easier, we will use the word *candidate* to refer to anyone in any phase of the process of initiation.

Understanding the Initiation Process

You are part of an ancient tradition of initiation in the Church. In the very early Church, adults who wished to become Christian underwent an extended period of formation and "probation" that was called a *catechumenate*. The heart of the catechumenate was conversion to Jesus Christ. It was a type of apprenticeship that included comprehensive training in the Christian way of life. Members of the Christian community were actively involved in teaching those who wanted to join the community. Members of the community were role models of the Christian way of life. Their words, deeds and actions drew others to this life. Community members also served as teachers and sponsors.

Sometime during the fifth century the catechumenate began to lose its importance. Large numbers of people were coming into the Church and infant Baptism was becoming the norm. By the Middle Ages there was no catechumenate at all. Then, for many reasons, including a renewed emphasis on evangelization and mission, the Second Vatican Council (1962-1965) called for reinstating the catechumenate for initiating adults (and children who had reached the age of reason) into the Catholic Church. Thus, in 1972 Pope Paul VI promulgated the *Rite of Christian Initiation of Adults*. In 1988, the bishops of the United States made the use of the Rite mandatory for all their parishes.

Many parishes began their use of the Rite in the early 1970's. Others have only recently begun to implement it. Nonetheless, the wisdom and tradition contained in the Rite is rich and inspiring.

Let's take a brief walk through this important Church document so that you will understand how the role of sponsor fits into the vision and structure of initiation as described in the Rite.

The Vision and Structure of the Rite

First, the vision of Christian initiation as presented to us in the Rite is that initiation is first and foremost a journey of conversion to our loving God in Jesus Christ. The Church tells us that "initiation is suited to a spiritual journey of adults that varies according to the many forms of God's grace" (*RCIA*, #5). People often begin this spiritual journey because they have a desire for "something more" in life. Frequently, adults and children are seeking the living God, even though they are not always able to articulate their needs and desire in the language of faith. The Rite describes the path to our loving God as a gradual, comprehensive and intense journey into the mystery of salvation. For many pilgrims, the journey culminates with the celebration of the Sacraments of

Baptism, Confirmation and Eucharist.

The pathway includes different periods of formation and liturgical rites along the way to mark the steps of those who seek God. The four periods of the initiation process and the liturgical rites along the way give structure to the process of initiation. They are described below:

The First Period:
EVANGELIZATION AND PRECATECHUMENATE

The first phase of the journey of initiation is the period of evangelization and precatechumenate. This is a time of seeking and questioning in which the candidate inquires about the Catholic faith. Hence, during this time candidates are often called *inquirers*. Inquirers come to the parish to find out more about God, Jesus, the Bible or the Church. They may come to Church because they find "something missing" in their lives, but they're not sure what it is. Or they may have been inspired by a friend or family member to find out more about the faith. But, regardless of the reason, they all come to us seeking something. We warmly welcome them and begin to walk with them during this initial period to help them find out what or whom they seek.

This period is a time for listening to those seekers. We listen to their questions, needs, wants and longings. We listen to their story and share our own story—the Christian story. We tell the story of salvation. We tell the Good News of Jesus Christ as it has been lived and proclaimed in Christian community throughout the ages. We tell how the Good News is being lived in the present, in our own lives, in our parish and our community. We also share our own, personal story of our faith life with Christ. Many inquirers will want to know how their sponsors were drawn to the Church and how their faith is lived.

For some, particularly those who have had no religious upbringing, the Good News of Jesus Christ and the story of our salvation are relatively unfamiliar. Many of those who come to us have no sense of a relationship with Jesus Christ. This period allows inquirers to develop that relationship and to develop an initial commitment to the Christian community and the Christian way of life.

In other situations, however, the person inquiring may already be quite familiar with the Good News of Jesus Christ. Such a person is already "evangelized," meaning that he or she already has a relationship with Christ and perhaps even a commitment to the Christian way of life. Frequently, this inquirer is a baptized candidate from another Christian tradition who wishes to join the Roman Catholic Church. In this instance, the period of evangelization and precatechumenate may be relatively short—it may not even be necessary at all. After the period of evangelization and precatechumenate, the candidate moves to the second period of the initiation process. The Church celebrates and ritualizes this step on the journey of initiation. For the unbaptized, the first ritual in the initiation process is called the Rite of Acceptance Into the Order of Catechumens.

The First Step:
THE RITE OF ACCEPTANCE INTO
THE ORDER OF CATECHUMENS

The first step in the process of Christian initiation is the celebration of the Rite of Acceptance Into the Order of Catechumens. (By "step" we mean a liturgical rite that marks a person's movement from one period to the next.) Having undergone an initial conversion to Jesus Christ and having a desire to live the Christian way of life, the inquirer passes into the second period of the initiation process.

The Rite of Acceptance Into the Order of Catechumens is a major celebration for inquirers. Through this rite, the Church publicly recognizes their initial conversion. The inquirers are now called "catechumens." They have accepted the gospel and expressed their desire to learn more about the word of God and the Christian way of life.

During the Rite of Acceptance Into the Order of Catechumens, the sponsor presents the inquirer to the parish community. Further, the sponsor promises to help the new catechumen to know and follow Jesus Christ. The rite also marks the beginning of the second period, the *catechumenate*. The sponsor accompanies the catechumen throughout this entire second period.

There is a similar rite for those who are already baptized. It is called the Rite of Welcoming Candidates. This rite welcomes candidates into the life of the community and marks the beginning of their period of formal preparation for the Sacraments of Confirmation and Eucharist. If they have had little religious formation, their period of preparation may be very similar to the preparation of catechumens.

The Second Period:
THE CATECHUMENATE

During the catechumenate period, catechumens learn more about the word of God, the teachings of the Church, the community, prayer and apostolic works of service for others. It is a time to deepen their conversion to Jesus Christ and the Christian way of life. The catechumenate may be an extended period of time depending upon the progress of the catechumen.

Those who are already baptized may enter a period of formation similar to the catechumenate. However, the baptized are not called catechumens, but rather "candidates." That is, they are candidates for reception into the full communion of the Catholic Church. Or, they are Catholics who are candidates for Confirmation and Eucharist. In some parishes, catechumens and candidates may meet together regularly and even celebrate the liturgical rites together. In other parishes, catechumens and baptized candidates may meet separately, depending upon the needs of each.

During the catechumenate, the formation the catechumens receive is based upon the word of God proclaimed during Sunday Mass. In many parishes, the catechumens are dismissed after the Liturgy of the Word, that is, after the readings and the homily. After they are dismissed, they gather in another location with a *catechist* (teacher), who helps them better understand the Scripture readings and apply them to their lives. The dismissal is a liturgical rite that sends the catechumens forth to reflect upon God's word. It is a gesture of hospitality. Since catechumens cannot receive Communion, they are invited to feast upon God's word. In this way, they deepen their understanding of sacred Scripture and intensify their desire for the body and blood of Christ.

Often, there is some time of further teaching that goes on in addition to this. Sponsors usually do not attend the dismissal *catechesis* (teaching), but all participate in some type of catechesis.

In summary, the period of the catechumenate is a time for teaching. It also includes time for prayer, worship and works of justice and service. A good deal of a sponsor's time and effort is put forth during this period. A sponsor's official role *may* end as this period ends, deferring to the godparent, whose role begins at the next step.

This Christian initiation through the catechumenate should be the concern of not only catechists or priests, but the entire community of the faithful, especially the sponsors. Thus, right from the outset the catechumens will feel that they belong to the People of God. (*The Documents of Vatican II*, Decree on the Church's Missionary Activity, #14)

The Second Step:
THE RITE OF ELECTION

The Rite of Election is the culmination of the period of the catechumenate and the official beginning of the period of purification and enlightenment. The Rite of Election, usually celebrated on the First Sunday of Lent, marks the beginning of the final, intense period of preparation for the catechumens. With the celebration of this rite, the catechumens are now called the "elect," because they have been elected by God through the Church to receive the Sacraments of Initiation: Baptism, Confirmation and Eucharist. In some areas, the elect from all the parishes in a diocese come together for this rite, with the bishop presiding. Sometimes, sponsors attend as well.

This rite begins the final period of intense, spiritual preparation for the sacraments that will be received at the Easter Vigil. During this rite, the Church affirms the catechumens' readiness to receive the Sacraments of Initiation. This is the step in which the catechumens enroll their name in the book that lists all those who have been chosen for Baptism (*RCIA*, #119).

Prior to the Rite of Election the catechumens choose godparents. The godparents present the catechumens at the rite and give testimony on their behalf. The parish sponsor may or may not be chosen by the catechumen to be the godparent.

Baptized candidates may celebrate a rite similar to the Rite of Election. It is known as the Rite of Calling the Candidates to Continuing Conversion. This rite also begins their period of final spiritual preparation for the sacraments.

The Third Period:
PURIFICATION AND ENLIGHTENMENT

The period of purification and enlightenment is the time of spiritual recollection for the sacraments. The nature of this period is much different from that of the previous period. Whereas the previous period was about doctrinal and pastoral formation, this time is about interior spiritual reflection and preparation for the Easter mysteries.

This period usually coincides with Lent and therefore has much of a Lenten character and flavor. It is a time of baptismal preparation and penitential renewal. Rather than focusing on catechesis and teaching, the elect focus on the celebration of rites called scrutinies and presentations. These are liturgical rituals that bring about their purification and enlightenment (*RCIA*, #139). The scrutinies are rituals of self-searching and repentance which complete the conversion of the elect (*RCIA*, #141). The scrutinies are celebrated on the third, fourth and fifth Sundays of Lent. The presentations of the Creed and the Lord's Prayer, which may take place on a weekday, enlighten the minds of the elect. There may also be rituals for the baptized candidates during this period.

The conclusion of this period at the end of the Lenten season brings us to the sacred days of Holy Thursday, Good Friday and Holy Saturday.

The Third Step:
THE CELEBRATION OF THE SACRAMENTS OF INITIATION

At the Easter Vigil on Holy Saturday, the elect will be baptized into the mystery of Christ. They will be sealed with the sacred chrism in Confirmation. And they will culminate their journey at the banquet table as they receive the Holy Eucharist. Only in exceptional circumstances is the celebration of the Sacraments of Initiation held outside of the Easter Vigil.

Baptized candidates who are being received into the full communion of the Catholic Church may celebrate the Rite of Reception and celebrate Confirmation and Eucharist at the Easter Vigil. Or, their reception and celebration of the sacraments may be at a time other than the Easter Vigil. Likewise, baptized Catholics may celebrate Confirmation and Eucharist at a time other than Easter.

Whether the sacramental celebrations are at the Easter Vigil or at another time, a final period of catechesis follows the sacramental celebration. This period after Baptism is called *mystagogy.*

The Fourth Period:
MYSTAGOGY

Mystagogy is an ancient word that refers to mystery. Here, mystagogy means the unpacking, unlocking and reflecting upon the sacred mysteries known as sacraments. This period is a time for the newly baptized to reflect upon the meaning of the sacraments they have recently received. Having been immersed into the mystery of salvation at the Easter Vigil, the newly baptized spend time exploring the meaning of their new life in Christ. Mystagogy helps these *neophytes* to fully appreciate and participate in the Christian community of which they have become a part.

The neophytes do the unpacking or unfolding of the Easter sacraments in several ways. First, they spend time reflecting upon the meaning, significance, beauty and power of the Easter Vigil. Time is afforded for them to talk about what the celebration of the sacraments meant to them. They explore the meaning of the sacraments and how the sacraments affect their lives.

Another way the neophytes deepen their understanding of the Easter sacraments is by their participation in the Sunday Eucharist. Now that they are fully initiated Catholic Christians, they celebrate the fullness of the Holy Eucharist each Sunday. This is an especially rich and meaningful time for them to celebrate the sacrament for which they have longed. Each Sunday of the Easter season the newly baptized are invited to reflect upon the mystery of the Body of Christ of which they are now a part. They are also invited to pay special attention to the Scripture readings of the Easter season. The Scripture readings that we hear at Mass are especially important for the new members of the Church. Neophytes often gather after Mass each week in Easter to talk about their new experiences.

Thirdly, the time of mystagogy is a time for neophytes to fully embrace and live out their mission of discipleship. Now that they are united to Jesus Christ in Baptism, they share in the mission of Jesus Christ. They now have a responsibility to put into action the promise they made to live as Christ would live. The parish community helps the neophytes to live in the world as a baptized follower of Jesus.

Lastly, the formal period of mystagogy coincides with the fifty days of the Easter Season. However, the extended period of mystagogy lasts to at least the next Easter (*RCIA*, National Statute, #24). If the baptized candidates celebrate the Sacraments of Initiation outside of the Easter season, a time of mystagogy must be included so they, too, can unfold the holy mysteries they have received.

For Reflection and Discussion

- *How were you asked to be a sponsor for the RCIA? Why did you accept?*

- *What concerns or questions do you have about being a sponsor?*

- *The RCIA is often called a journey of conversion. What kind of images or feelings does the concept of "journey" have for you?*

- *Conversion may be described as a "turning away" from something and a "turning toward" something else. Name a time when you "turned away" from something and "turned toward" something else. (For example: You turned away from over-working and turned toward family and self.)*

The rite of initiation is suited to a spiritual journey of adults that varies according to the many forms of God's grace, the free cooperation of individuals, the action of the Church, and the circumstances of time and place. (*RCIA*, #5)

We have found the Messiah: Jesus Christ, who brings us truth and grace. (John 1:41, 17b. As given in the *Rite of Acceptance Into the Order of Catechumens*, #62)

From the time of the apostles, becoming a Christian has been accomplished by a journey and initiation in several stages. This journey can be covered rapidly or slowly, but certain essential elements will always have to be present: proclamation of the Word, acceptance of the Gospel entailing conversion, profession of faith, Baptism itself, the outpouring of the Holy Spirit, and admission to the Eucharistic communion. (*Catechism of the Catholic Church*, #1229)

The Holy Mysteries: The Sacraments of Initiation

The culmination of the entire process of Christian initiation is the celebration of the Sacraments of Initiation: Baptism, Confirmation and Eucharist. Let's take some time to look at each of these holy mysteries, or sacraments, of the Church.

Baptism

United With Christ. In Baptism we are united with Jesus Christ. As we go down into the saving waters (or as the water is poured over us) we are made one with Christ. Just as surely as Jesus descended to the dead after his crucifixion and then rose to new life, we unite ourselves with Christ in the mystery of death and resurrection when we "go down" into the waters of Baptism. Thus, in Baptism we share in the death and the resurrection of Jesus Christ. Through the power of the holy water our lives become one with the life of Jesus Christ. As such, we share in all the promises of Christ. Most importantly, we share in the promise of everlasting life.

To symbolize the everlasting life and light of Christ that burns within us we are given a candle at Baptism. The flame of the candle is taken from the flame of the Easter candle or Paschal candle. The Paschal candle represents the light of Christ. As the flame of our baptismal candle has as its source the light of Christ, so too, the source of our life is Christ.

A New Creation. In Baptism we are made a new creation. The life-giving waters of Baptism give us new life. The waters of life wash away the "old" and give us the "new." In Baptism, we leave behind our "old" former and sinful ways of living and we accept the way of Jesus Christ. The sinful ways of our past are washed away and made clean and new. Everything that is sinful or evil is wiped out by the power-filled waters of Baptism. What remains is a new creation. This new creation is free from all sin. As Catholics we believe we are freed from original sin. Sin is wiped out and we begin life anew.

To symbolize our new life in Christ, we are given a white garment. The white garment is a sign of our new life, our freedom from sin, and our unity with Christ.

Adopted as God's Children. In Baptism we are adopted as God's children. In Baptism, we celebrate our rebirth as God's own daughters and sons. We have been born of this earth by our human parents, and in Baptism we are born again, or made new, as God's children. As God's adopted children, we share in the inheritance of our brother, Jesus Christ. We share in the inheritance of the eternal life that he won for us by his death and resurrection.

In Baptism we are made into God's own people. That is, we become one of God's chosen ones. We become part of the people of God, the Church. In Baptism, we are incorporated into the life of Christ and also into the life of the Church. We become members of the Body of Christ.

In summary, through the power of the holy waters of Baptism we are united forever with Jesus Christ. We are made one with Christ and share in the mystery of his life, death and resurrection. The life-giving waters of Baptism free us from sin and make us a new creation. We are given a new life as God's adopted daughters and sons.

Confirmation

Confirmation is the second Sacrament of Initiation. It is closely connected to Baptism and includes an anointing with chrism that is similar to the post-baptismal anointing for infants.

Full Outpouring of the Holy Spirit. Although we receive the gift of the Holy Spirit at our Baptism, we believe that through the Sacrament of Confirmation we receive the full outpouring of the Holy Spirit. The Holy Spirit gives us strength to live as disciples of Jesus Christ and guides us on the way.

In addition to receiving strength and guidance from the Holy Spirit, we are given all the gifts of the Holy Spirit. We receive "the spirit of wisdom and understanding, the spirit of right judgment and courage, the spirit of knowledge and reverence…, the spirit of wonder and awe" (*Rite of Confirmation*, #25).

As the bishop or priest lays hands upon us, he prays that we will receive the many gifts of the spirit. Since ancient times, the laying on of hands has been a sign for calling the Holy Spirit upon a person.

Made More Like Christ. In Confirmation we are also anointed with the holy oil of chrism. We are anointed to be more like Christ. In Baptism, we are united with Christ, then by being anointed with oil in Confirmation we are made even more like our savior. Through the sacred oil of chrism we are in a sense shaped or molded or "configured" to be like Jesus Christ.

What was begun in Baptism is now "sealed" in the anointing of Confirmation. As the bishop or priest signs us with the oil he says, "Be sealed with the Gift of the Holy Spirit" (*Rite of Confirmation*, #27).

In summary, in the Sacrament of Confirmation the laying on of hands symbolizes our being filled with the gifts of the Holy Spirit. Furthermore, we are anointed with the holy oil of chrism and thereby made to be more like Christ, priest, prophet and king.

Eucharist

The Holy Eucharist is the culminating point of Christian initiation. Having been washed clean in Baptism and made to be more like Christ in Confirmation, the person now comes to the eucharistic table to receive the bread and wine of everlasting life and to go forth in mission. The word *Eucharist* refers to "communion"—when we receive the body and blood of Jesus Christ. *Eucharist* also refers to the Catholic Mass in its entirety.

The Bread of Life. In the Eucharist we receive the body and blood of Jesus Christ. We believe that through the power of the Holy Spirit the bread and wine offered at Mass become the body and blood of Jesus Christ. We believe the Eucharist is our bread of life. By receiving the bread and wine of everlasting life we are given the strength and nourishment we need to live as faithful disciples of Jesus Christ.

A Memorial Sacrifice. In the Eucharist, or at Mass, we recall the great sacrifice that Jesus made for us. We recall the Last Supper where Jesus offered his own body and blood for us. We remember and give thanks for Jesus' death and resurrection. Not only do we remember, but also when we gather together at Mass for this memorial sacrifice, we make Christ Jesus actually present with us. We believe that by sacrificing himself on the cross Jesus won for us the forgiveness of our sins. By his death and resurrection he won our salvation.

In addition, we believe in the *real presence* of Jesus Christ in the bread and the wine. We also believe that Christ is present in the assembly of believers, in the priest and in the Word of God proclaimed at Mass.

A Sacred Meal. The Eucharist is also a holy meal. As Catholic Christians we gather around the table to remember Jesus' life, death and resurrection. Scripture is read, wine is poured and bread is broken. By sharing in the body and blood of Christ, we are united with one another and with Christ Jesus our Lord. By sharing in the flesh of Christ, we are united not only to him, but also to one another. Sharing the body of Christ strengthens us *to be* the Body of Christ.

We are sent forth from this sacred meal strengthened and nourished that we might continue the work Jesus began on earth. The Eucharist sends us forth in mission. United with Christ and with one another we have the strength and courage to continue to minister to others.

In summary, Eucharist is the bread of life. It is the body and blood of Christ Jesus our Savior. In Eucharist we give praise and thanks for the great sacrifice Jesus made for our salvation. We commemorate the great sacrifice Jesus made for us. We remember and celebrate by sharing in a sacred meal. And, finally strengthened by Christ's own body and blood, we are sent forth in mission for the life of the world.

For Reflection and Discussion

- *In the description of the Sacraments of Baptism, Confirmation and Eucharist, what phrase, image or symbol struck you or got your attention?*

- *What image comes to mind when you think of your own Baptism? Spend some time thinking or writing about this. At some point in time, share these thoughts and feelings with your candidate.*

- *When did you celebrate the Sacrament of Confirmation? What memory do you have of the celebration?*

- *What meaning did the Sacrament of Confirmation have for you then? What meaning does it have for you now?*

- *Eucharist is a weekly celebration, for some it is even daily. Why do you celebrate Eucharist? What is most powerful for you about the Eucharist?*

Thus the three sacraments of Christian initiation closely combine to bring us, the faithful of Christ, to his full stature and to enable us to carry out the mission of the entire people of God in the Church and in the world. (*Christian Initiation,* "General Introduction," #2d)

Do you not know that all of us who have been baptized into Christ Jesus were baptized into his death? We were buried therefore with him by Baptism into death, so that as Christ was raised from the dead by the glory of the Father, we too might walk in newness of life. (Romans 6:3-4)

Since the beginning of the church, adult Baptism is the common practice where the proclamation of the Gospel is still new. The catechumenate (preparation for Baptism) therefore occupies an important place. This initiation into Christian faith and life should dispose the catechumen to receive the gift of God in Baptism, Confirmation, and the Eucharist. (*Catechism of the Catholic Church,* #1247)

The Role of the Sponsor

As a sponsor in the RCIA, you have a vital role in the Church's ministry of initiation. You have a variety of roles and responsibilities. In this section, we'll look at those responsibilities from the Church's point of view. We'll help you to better understand what your parish is asking of you. In the next section, we'll give you some practical suggestions for being a good and effective sponsor.

A companion is one who accompanies another on a journey. In this case, the journey is to a deeper relationship with God in Jesus Christ through the Holy Spirit. The journey takes place in the midst of the Christian community. *You* are a representative of the Christian community. Let's explore a little further what it means to "accompany" another in the midst of a Christian community.

Imagine for a moment, accompanying another person on a magnificently beautiful, forested, mountainous hike. Imagine the terrain to be fabulously picturesque, yet rugged, even treacherous, at times. The hike leads to a breathtakingly stunning mountain peak—a view to die for! You are quite familiar with the pathway that leads to the peak. You have traveled the path many times and are sure-footed and confident. Though you, too, stumble and fall at times, you know the way.

You are the guide on this journey. You accompany your companion, not just in the sense of "walking beside" the person, but you guide your companion along the pathway. You point out the scenic overlooks—the important spots. You also help your companion when the going gets tough. You may have to lend a hand or help him with his footing. You encourage your companion when he gets discouraged or confused. Though you are not the teacher (there is a lead hiker who does the teaching), you certainly offer your own insights and personal experiences of hiking as you move along the pathway.

Furthermore, there are others on this path with you. The two of you are not walking alone. There are people of various ages and backgrounds on the journey up the mountain, too. Everyone travels at a different pace, with a different set of skills and abilities; nonetheless, you travel together. You learn from, support and encourage one another along the way.

A Companion

This imaginary mountaintop hike illustrates the companioning role of a sponsor. First, a companion is one who accompanies a person in a very proactive sense—more than a passive "walk beside me." When one accompanies another, you enhance and complement the journey. As a sponsor, your own experience of being a Catholic Christian can serve to complement a candidate's journey. Sharing your own story of living the Catholic Christian way of life helps the candidate to better understand where she is on the journey.

A Guide

Second, a sponsor is a guide. A guide is a type of "veteran." You are a veteran in the sense that you have walked the walk. You have walked the pathway as a Catholic Christian. You are familiar with the Catholic territory. A guide helps a candidate to understand the territory. The Catholic Christian way of life may be quite unfamiliar to some people. The sponsor helps the candidate to understand the Catholic Christian terrain, not by being a teacher, but by walking beside the person and sharing experiences as you move along.

As a guide, you help the candidate to navigate through unfamiliar waters. You guide the candidate through parish life. You walk with the candidate through the ins and outs of what's happening in the parish. You'll want to explain some traditions of your parish. You'll want not only to explain but also to participate in some social and service activities of the parish. You'll also be expected to participate with your candidate in the worship life of the parish, which includes Sunday Mass as well as other forms of prayer such as Morning Prayer and Evening Prayer or other types of prayer your parish may offer. Sitting next to a trusted companion as we worship our loving God can give a sense of comfort and peace.

A Representative of
the Christian Community

Furthermore, as a sponsor you represent the larger parish community. As you guide your candidate along the pathway, you and your candidate are connected to the larger Christian community. You do not work alone. You are the candidate's personal connection to the Roman Catholic Church, both to the local parish and to the Church universal. When an inquirer comes to the Church seeking initiation, he or she is welcomed by individual parishioners, not by an anonymous parish. In fact, often it is an inquirer's previous association with or friendship with a parishioner that initially draws him or her to the Church. One-to-one contact makes the Church feel real, human and personal.

Sometimes a parish can seem large and impersonal. It's pretty easy to walk in and out of church and not talk to anyone. But, as the sponsor, you are the friendly face that will always (or at least usually) be there when your candidate comes to church. Whether it is to one of the RCIA sessions, Sunday Mass, the parish festival, Advent evening prayer or the Lenten fish fry, you help the candidate to feel comfortable in these settings. That is not to say that you must attend every parish function. However, you want to be sure your candidate feels at home in various parish settings. Help him or her become acquainted with other parishioners and encourage fellow parishioners to reach out to new candidates.

As the representative of the Catholic Christian community, your candidate is likely to turn to you with questions or concerns. You are *not* expected to know the answer to every Catholic question a candidate may ask. Be honest! Tell your candidate when you don't know the answer. The catechists, priests and initiation coordinator will answer those questions. Simply speak from your heart and speak from your experience when you respond to your candidate's questions. However, also be aware that you represent the Roman Catholic Church. You need to be forthright, clear and consistent about what the Church teaches and believes. When you are unsure, ask the coordinator or a catechist for assistance.

Another way to think about the Christian community you represent is to think of the parish as the mentor and the candidate as the apprentice. A mentor is a wise and accomplished master or teacher. The apprentice is the newcomer who wants to learn a new skill, trade or occupation. In this case, the newcomer wants to learn not a skill or trade but a whole way of life. The apprentice learns the Christian way of life from the mentor. The mentor is the entire parish. It is the parish that shows the apprentice how to live as a disciple of Jesus Christ. You, as the sponsor, are the vital link between the candidate and the mentoring community.

The relationship between the mentor and the apprentice is unique. The mentor teaches the apprentice not so much through traditional instruction but by working with the apprentice: teaching by doing, living the life. The candidate learns the Christian way of life by living in the midst of the community—studying and learning the teachings and traditions of the Church. It means praying and socializing with members of the parish. It means worshipping with the assembly gathered on Sunday. It means doing apostolic works of justice and service alongside the faithful.

As you can see, there is a lot for the apprentice to learn from the mentor. Fortunately, the mentor is an entire community, not just the sponsor. The Second Vatican Council described the apprenticeship of a catechumen in this way:

> The catechumenate is not a mere expounding of doctrines and precepts, but a training period for the whole Christian life. It is an apprenticeship of appropriate length, during which disciples are joined to Christ their teacher. (*Decree on the Church's Missionary Activity,* #14)

So, relax. You do not have to teach your candidate a whole way of life! It's the job of the community to train the apprentice and Christ is the teacher. The Church is the Body of Christ. Your job as sponsor is to help the candidate find plenty of opportunities to interact, worship, work, play, serve and pray with the community.

A Witness

In the earliest days of the Church, if someone wanted to join the Church, a community member had to bring the person forward and testify as to her sincerity and good intention. The sponsor had to testify that the person was a suitable candidate. After this sort of "sponsor" testified on behalf of the potential candidate, then the person could be admitted to a period of formation in the Christian way of life.[1] This ancient tradition continues in

[1] Paul Turner, *The Hallelujah Highway: A History of the Catechumenate* (Chicago: Liturgy Training Publications, 2000) p. 38.

a modified form today.

Indeed, the Church today describes sponsors as "persons who have known and assisted the candidates and stand as witnesses to the candidates' moral character, faith and intention" (*RCIA,* #10). When determining if a person is ready for more serious instruction and formation in the Catholic Christian way of life, the parish relies on the sponsor, to some extent, to give input as to the candidate's disposition. The parish looks to the sponsor to give an indication as to whether or not the candidate is sincerely searching for God and longing for a deeper relationship with Christ in the Church. If the sponsor, along with the catechists and priest feel that the person is ready to proceed on the pathway toward full sacramental initiation, then the inquirer is admitted to the Order of Catechumens. In other words, when the Church decides the person is ready, the inquirer celebrates the Rite of Acceptance Into the Order of Catechumens. Thus, they begin the second and more formal period of their Christian formation, called the period of the catechumenate (see above).

Some sponsors feel uncomfortable with "witnessing" as to someone else's character and intention. They may ask themselves, "Who am I to judge?" However, the emphasis is not on judging a person's innermost heart and soul. The sponsor's responsibility is to give input so that the pastor can decide if this inquirer is ready to enter a time of pastoral formation. The Church takes the formation of new Christians very seriously. The pastor has a responsibility to earnestly consider who is admitted to our most holy sacraments. Since sponsors spend time getting to know inquirers, they are asked to help in this first step of discernment.

Usually, the testimony you give about your candidate will be done within the familiar, comfortable and confidential setting of your RCIA group. Often, there is an evening of discernment where sponsors testify as to why they believe their inquirer is ready to become a catechumen or a candidate for reception into full communion with the Roman Catholic Church. In other situations, you may give testimony directly to the RCIA coordinator or to the pastor. In any case, the role of witness is an important and often powerful part of being a parish sponsor.

The Distinction Between a Sponsor and a Godparent

Your role as a parish sponsor usually begins sometime during the first period of the initiation process, the period of evangelization and precatechumenate. Your role continues up to the Rite of Election, which is the beginning of the third period. The candidate chooses godparents (a godmother or godfather, or both) to stand up at the Rite of Election. The godparent may or may not be the same person as the parish sponsor. A godparent and a parish sponsor are two different ministries.

The confusing part is that the Church sometimes calls godparents "Baptismal sponsors." And, there is also the tradition of Confirmation sponsors. Parish sponsors in the RCIA, godparents and Confirmation sponsors are all different. You may be a parish sponsor, or you may end up being all three! Let's distinguish among the three.

A godparent's role begins publicly at the Rite of Election. The godparents continue to accompany the candidates throughout the period of purification and enlightenment (which usually coincides with Lent), at the celebration of the Sacraments of Initiation and during the period of mystagogy (*RCIA,* #11). In summary, a parish sponsor accompanies a candidate through the first two periods of the initiation process. The godparents accompany the candidate through the final two periods of the process, and they continue their role as godparents throughout the rest of the candidate's Christian life.

Why do different people accompany a candidate at different times? Traditionally, the sponsor is the person who presents or brings the candidate—often a friend, neighbor or spouse—to the parish. When a person comes to the Church unaccompanied, the parish assigns a parish sponsor. Parish sponsors are chosen because they have the qualities needed to welcome a candidate and help through the initial periods of formation. They are not expected to make a lifelong commitment like a godparent.

The difference between the parish sponsor and the godparent is that the godparent stands with the candidate at the celebration of the sacraments. The godparent also has a lifelong commitment to help the person "persevere in faith and in their lives as Christians" ("General Introduction," *Christian Initiation,* #8). Also, the candidate chooses the godparent. At least one of the godparents must be a baptized, confirmed, practicing Roman Catholic in good standing with the Church. In addition to the Roman Catholic godparent, a baptized Christian from another Christian tradition can stand as a Christian witness.[2]

---

[2] A. Coriden, Thomas J. Green and Donald E. Heintschel, *The Code of Canon Law: A Text and Commentary* (New York: Paulist Press, 1985), canon 874, pp. 629-630.

Often relatives or friends who have been involved and supportive throughout a candidate's lifelong journey are chosen as the godparents. Mary chooses Aunt Millie from Timbuktu to be a godmother because she has been a model of the Christian way of life since Mary was a child. However, since Aunt Millie is not a member of your parish, she would obviously not make a good parish sponsor. Without a doubt, though, Great Aunt Millie will continue to support and encourage Mary wherever Mary's life journey may take her.

On the other hand, the parish asks the sponsor to make a limited commitment. We do not ask you to make a lifelong commitment. However, we certainly hope that the relationship and friendship you make with your candidate lasts a lifetime! Realistically, though, you or your candidate may move away from your current parish. Your formal commitment will be ongoing only if your candidate asks you to be a godparent and you accept the responsibility.

Nonetheless, even if your official role as parish sponsor ends at the Rite of Election, the parish hopes that you have developed a Christian bonding with your candidate and that you will continue to support her or him on the journey. Often, godparents live out of town and cannot be present during the many rituals of the Lenten season. So, you may be asked to stand as proxy for a godparent.

Furthermore, your candidate may already have godparents. She may have been baptized in the Roman Catholic Church or in another tradition that recognizes the ministry of godparents. Traditionally, Roman Catholic godparents also stand as the sponsors for the Sacrament of Confirmation. However, if your candidate needs a sponsor for the Sacrament of Confirmation, you may be asked to stand up with your candidate when she or he is confirmed. Once again, however, note that being a sponsor for the Sacrament of Confirmation is different from being a parish RCIA sponsor.

In summary, as the parish sponsor your role is to be a companion, a guide, a representative of the community and a witness. You are part of an important and ancient tradition of bringing to the Church those who seek Christ.

For Reflection and Discussion

- *Recall a time in your life when you walked as a companion or guide with another person—maybe a trip with a friend, a colleague, a scout troop. What do you remember most about the experience?*

- *As one who represents your parish, what do you most want your candidate to know or experience about your parish? Name three things.*

- *What aspect of being a sponsor do you look forward to the most? Why?*

- *What aspect of being a sponsor will you find most challenging? Why? Would you like to talk to an RCIA team member about this?*

The people of God, as represented by the local Church, should understand and show by their concern that the initiation of adults is the responsibility of all the baptized. Therefore, the community must always be fully prepared in pursuit of its apostolic vocation to give help to those who are searching for Christ. In various circumstances of daily life...all the followers of Christ have the obligation of spreading the faith according to their abilities. (*RCIA, #9*)

That very day two of them were going to a village named Emmaus, about seven miles from Jerusalem, and talking with each other about all the things that had happened. While they were talking and discussing together, Jesus himself drew near and went with them. (Luke 24:13-15)

The catechumenate, or formation of catechumens, aims at bringing their conversion and faith to maturity, in response to the divine initiative and in union with an ecclesial community. (*Catechism of the Catholic Church, #1248*)

Qualities of a Sponsor

Sponsors come in lots of different shapes and sizes. Every sponsor is unique and has her or his own way of doing things. There is not one particular "type of person" that makes a good sponsor. There is not one particular way to be a good sponsor. Sponsors can be extroverts, introverts, single, married, divorced, rich, poor, young or old. Most importantly, a sponsor is an active, practicing Catholic who is willing to share faith and is free to carry out the responsibilities of sponsoring.

Notwithstanding, there are some qualities that make for a good sponsor. Considering the list of qualities given here may help you to become aware of some of those qualities that are hidden within you. Reviewing this list occasionally will help you to be more aware of how you can be an even better sponsor.

A sponsor has a willingness to share faith. A sponsor is a person who is willing to share with another person his faith, love, commitment and relationship with Jesus Christ. Talk with your candidate about what Jesus Christ means in your life. Talk about the simple ways in which you live your faith each day. In one way or another, your candidate is looking to begin or deepen her relationship with Jesus. Seeing your faith put into words and action can help the candidate further develop her own.

A sponsor is prayerful. A sponsor is a person of prayer. A sponsor has and knows the importance of having an active prayer life. Pray for and with your candidate. Talk about the way you pray, but also be aware of and sensitive to the many different ways of praying. Your candidate may need or want a style of prayer different from your own. You may need to actually "teach" your candidate to pray. Folks who are new to the Christian way of life are sometimes very unfamiliar with how to pray. Praying with you will help them to learn.

A sponsor is welcoming and hospitable. A good sponsor makes her candidate feel comfortable being in and around the parish. A sponsor has a sense of hospitality. Whether it's at an RCIA session, at Mass or at another parish function, go out of your way to make your candidate feel at home. Warmly greet your candidate each and every time you see him. Sit with him and talk to him at sessions. Believe it or not, lots of sponsors think that being in the same room with a candidate is enough. It's not! Go out of your way to reach out to your candidate. Remember he is new and may be a little bit uncertain or intimidated.

A sponsor is a good listener. All candidates come with a story. They have come to your parish and are in the initiation process for a reason. They are seeking God in one way or another, even though they might not say it in quite that language. Some people are very forthcoming with their story and their questions. Other candidates will be more reluctant to share. Be available to listen to your candidate's story. Sharing your story will help your candidate be more comfortable sharing her story. But remember, this is primarily about the candidate's story. Although sharing stories goes both ways, you should probably do more listening than talking.

Be open and attentive. There is no need to pry into a person's private matters, but be willing to really hear what is being said. And, be attentive to what may *not* be said. Sometimes what is not said or not asked can be very revealing. Be a kind and active listener, and be trustworthy enough to keep private matters confidential.

A sponsor is empathetic and compassionate. A sponsor is an understanding person. A sponsor tries to understand the feelings, concerns, joys, confusion and uncertainties of the candidate. There can be a wide range of emotions experienced on the journey of initiation. You need to be supportive and empathetic to whatever may be going on with your candidate. Some candidates come with a lot of "baggage" and issues they need to sort through. Though you are not expected to be, nor should you try to be a therapist, you can be compassionate about whatever is happening in the life of your candidate. If something serious arises, refer your candidate to the initiation coordinator or the pastor.

Sometimes a candidate needs a boost of encouragement. He or she may get negative feedback from family members or friends who do not understand or agree with the Catholic Christian way of life. Your candidate may get distracted or weary during the journey and wonder if it's really worth the effort. She may disagree with one of the teachings of the Church and need to discuss the issue with a trusted friend. Any number of situations may happen along the way. If you can be flexible, understanding and compassionate, you'll be a great sponsor!

A sponsor is informed. You'll help your candidate a great deal if you keep yourself informed—not only about what is happening in the parish, but also about what is happening in RCIA. Most candidates are not well-connected to the parish. They need you to help them know what is happening and what is important in the life of the parish. Just reading the bulletin and the parish newsletter will help you to stay informed.

Also, know what is happening in RCIA! Keep track of the schedule and the various events and liturgical rites. Help your candidate know where he needs to be, and when. Especially during the Lenten season there are many liturgical rites at various places and times. Even though you may not be the godparent, you'll do your candidate a great service if you can help him stay in touch with what is happening and why. Talk to your initiation coordinator or pastor whenever you need information or clarification.

A sponsor is willing to challenge. There may be a time when you need to challenge your candidate. For example, if your candidate shows a lack of commitment in attendance at Mass or at the RCIA sessions, you should kindly ask about the situation. Or, you may notice something in the attitude or actions of your candidate that is not in accord with the Catholic Christian way of life. Consult your initiation coordinator or pastor about the best way to discuss the matter with your candidate.

A sponsor is more than a Catholic cheerleader who cheers for the candidate no matter what happens. Sometimes, a person finds out that the Roman Catholic Church is not for her. You may help to set free a person who is struggling with making a decision for Catholicism. A candidate may feel obliged to "become Catholic" because a fiancé or spouse is Catholic. You may help to give them the freedom they need. Your honesty and willingness to talk about potential conflicts will help to ensure the spiritual well-being and best interests of the candidate and the Church.

A sponsor is a person of mission. As a parish sponsor, you share in the mission of Jesus Christ. You are helping to bring others into communion with our loving God. That is an awesome responsibility. Take it seriously. Moreover, your sense of mission will be contagious. You'll help your candidate to discover her role in the mission of the Church when she becomes a baptized member in full communion with the Roman Catholic Church.

For Reflection and Discussion

- *What is the greatest gift you bring to the ministry of sponsor?*

- *In what area could you use some development? What could the parish do to help you develop the skills or qualities you need?*

Then the sponsors and the whole congregation join in the following...

These catechumens, who are our brothers and sisters, have already traveled a long road. We rejoice with them in the gentle guidance of God who has brought them to this day. Let us pray that they may press onwards, until they come to share fully in our way of life. (*RCIA,* "Rite of Acceptance Into the Order of Catechumens," #65)

Now the Lord said to Abram, "Go from your country and your kindred and your father's house to the land that I will show you." (Genesis 12:1)

Thus formed, "the newly converted set out on a spiritual journey. Already sharing through faith in the mystery of Christ's death and resurrection, they pass from the old to a new nature made perfect in Christ. Since this transition brings with it a progressive change of outlook and conduct, it should become manifest by means of its social consequences and it should develop gradually during the catechumenate. Since the Lord in whom they believe is a sign of contradiction, the newly converted often experience divisions and separations, but they also taste the joy that God gives without measure." (*The Documents of Vatican II,* Decree on the Church's Missionary Activity, #13, as translated in *Rite of Christian Initiation of Adults,* #75.2)

Some Practical Suggestions

In some ways, being a sponsor for a candidate is just like being a friend to someone. It's simple! Right? You're introduced to someone and you become friends. But, just like developing any new friendship, it takes some time and effort. It's not always simple, but definitely worthwhile! Besides, there is more to being a sponsor than just "being a friend." So, here are some practical, parish-tested suggestions for some things you can do to develop, then deepen your relationship with your candidate.

In the Beginning:
THE PERIOD OF EVANGELIZATION AND PRECATECHUMENATE

Spend time welcoming. When you first meet the candidate you're going to sponsor, spend some time making him feel welcome. First, that means just spend some time getting acquainted. Be sure you have his telephone number and address. Send him a note or a card to say welcome to the parish if he is new. Be sure he has all the basic parish information. Since he is not Catholic, he may not be registered in the parish, so he won't get the regular parish mailings and newsletters.

Invite him to meet you for coffee and doughnuts after Mass. Remember, if he is a new inquirer, he may not be going to Mass regularly. Be aware of that and invite him to meet you for Mass followed by coffee or breakfast.

Go to the sessions. One of the most important things you can do is "be there." Be there when there is an RCIA session. Whether you meet on Wednesday night or Sunday morning, having your friendly face there at those initial sessions is very important. It speaks volumes when you make the time to go every single week. Or, at least most weeks! And, sit with your candidate. This may be a new environment for her, so help her to feel at home. Try not to get caught up chatting with your long-time parish friends. Focus on your candidate. Bring her into your conversations with other people.

Introduce the candidate to parish life. Introduce your candidate to other parishioners and to the life of the parish. Part of becoming Catholic is getting to know the parish beyond the RCIA group. Remember that most people don't like to go to functions or special events by themselves. No one wants to walk into a room or a church cold! When there is a prayer, social or service event happening in the parish, ask your candidate to meet you there. Or, offer to pick him up, if that's possible. Don't assume he knows what's happening and will get there on his own. He won't! Remember, welcoming and inviting are key at this stage.

Pray, pray, pray. Pray for your candidate. You may not know each other well enough at the beginning to pray together. But you can pray for your candidate. And, you'll pray with the group at your sessions. Begin to casually talk to your candidate about prayer. Maybe she already has a well-developed prayer life and would be quite comfortable praying with you. Or, maybe you're not quite comfortable. Praying together may take time to develop. Give it a try. Start out with simple, traditional prayers and then move to praying spontaneously. You may find it's easier than you thought.

One of the most important times for you to pray with your candidate is before one of the liturgical rites. The liturgical rites are major moments in the candidates' journey. Pray together before the rite to help the candidate discern whether she is ready. If so, pray for openness to God speaking and working in the ritual.

Remember Baptism. If your candidate is already baptized, encourage and help your candidate to find out about her Baptism. Help her do the research if need be. Meanwhile, find out about your own Baptism. Discuss with your candidate the meaning and significance of her Baptism. Talk about how this journey is a continuation of the journey begun at Baptism. Work with your initiation coordinator to develop ways to highlight your candidate's Baptism.

In the Middle:
THE PERIOD OF THE CATECHUMENATE

During the period of the catechumenate, your candidate is learning more about the teachings, traditions and life of the Church. Here are some things you can do to support this catechumenal experience:

- Attend the RCIA sessions.
- If your parish has dismissal of catechumens and candidates, meet your candidate after Mass and occasionally check in to find out how this "dismissal catechesis" is going.
- Invite your candidate to work at the St. Vincent de Paul Society with you.
- Take your candidate to visit some other Catholic churches, your cathedral and/or other Catholic agencies or institutions in your area.
- Go to a Christian bookstore (check ahead of time to see if they have some Catholic materials available).
- Sit together in silent prayer.
- Invite your candidate (and her or his family) to your home.
- Take a walk in the park together.
- Visit a parish shut in, or a senior citizen home.
- Go out for coffee or ice cream.
- Pray the rosary together (you may need to teach it, if a catechist hasn't).
- Attend a parish function together.
- If you are sponsoring a family with child candidates, go to the child's soccer game or science fair.
- Find a book of saints at the library and help your candidate find out about his namesake.

- Celebrate your candidate's birthday or patron saint's feast day.

- Send a card just to say, "Praying for you."

- Encourage your candidate to start her own Advent tradition by sharing one of yours. Adopt a needy family together during the holidays or at another time.

- Work at the parish carnival or fish fry together.

- Attend one of the meetings of your parish Justice and Peace Committee.

- Have fun! Do something that both of you enjoy doing. If you are sponsoring a family with children, do something the children enjoy, too.

This list could go on indefinitely. It can be as expansive as your imagination.

Also, check in occasionally to see if your candidate is satisfied with the process. Every once in a while simply ask, "How's it going?" Provide your candidate with the opportunity to express satisfaction as well as dissatisfaction or confusion. At times it's hard to know how your candidate is feeling unless you ask.

The Final Preparation:
THE PERIOD OF PURIFICATION AND ENLIGHTENMENT

If you are asked to be the candidate's godparent, you will have a very active role during the period of purification and enlightenment, usually during Lent. As a godparent, you'll be expected to do the following during the Lenten season:

- Stand up with your candidate at the Rite of Election.
- Stand up with your candidate during the three scrutinies.
- Participate in the preparation sessions for the scrutinies.
- Possibly attend the weekday celebrations of the Presentations of the Creed and the Lord's Prayer.
- Possibly attend a Lenten retreat.
- Pray a lot!
- Be attentive to the needs of the candidate as Easter Vigil draws near.
- Participate in the Holy Week liturgies with your candidate.
- Make or buy a card or gift to give to your candidate after Easter Vigil at the reception.
- Participate in the Preparation Rites on Holy Saturday.
- Stand up with your candidate at the Easter Vigil (or at another time if your candidate is already baptized).

If you are not the godparent, you do not have an official role to play once the period of the catechumenate closes. However, there is no reason why you can't call to see how he is doing, or invite him for a cup of coffee. And it is a wonderful gesture of support for you to go to the Rite of Election, even though you will not be standing up with your candidate. It's also a good idea to be present in the assembly at the Masses when your candidate celebrates the scrutinies. And, of course, participate in the Easter Vigil to celebrate the sacraments with your candidate.

The Final Period:
MYSTAGOGY

If you are asked to be the godparent, your role continues throughout the period of mystagogy. Mystagogy is the period of post-Baptismal formation. During this time, you'll help the newly baptized, the neophyte, to live his new life as a disciple of Jesus Christ. You'll continue to walk with him as he explores the meaning of the holy mysteries he has received. You'll help him to live as one incorporated into the Body of Christ. You'll support him as he finds his role in the mission of the Church.

One of the best things you can do is to talk with your neophyte about the beauty, power and meaning of the Easter Vigil. Talk about some of those peak moments of the Vigil when you were moved beyond words, when your eyes filled with tears, when you were covered with goose-bumps or when you simply felt touched by the Vigil.

Also, celebrate Eucharist with your neophyte. The context of mystagogy is Sunday Eucharist. During the Easter season make a special effort to sit with your neophyte during Mass. Afterward, talk about the experience. Talk about the readings of the Easter season. They are especially chosen for the newly initiated members of the Church. Talk about how it feels to now receive Eucharist after such a long period of preparation and fasting. Mystagogy happens primarily through Eucharist. Your godchild has received Eucharist and now learns to live it. Your continued example will be a great support.

In addition, you may need to encourage your neophyte to attend the RCIA sessions, which occur after Easter. Many neophytes experience an understandable letdown after the climax of Easter. Keeping in touch with the neophyte immediately after Easter will help. Knowing you will be going to the sessions will help, too!

Lastly, mystagogy lasts a lifetime for all the baptized. We, the faithful continue to deepen our grasp of the Paschal Mystery. We search for ways to better live out our baptismal commitment. If you are a godparent, your role as a support and guide lasts a lifetime, too. Yet, all of us, all the faithful have a responsibility to support and encourage our newest members. We are one body in Christ Jesus our Lord.

For Reflection and Discussion

- *What do you think and feel about making time to spend with your candidate? What do you anticipate enjoying the most? The least?*

- *List what you want to do and discuss with your candidate. Put your list on the refrigerator.*

- *In what way is being a sponsor living out your baptismal commitment?*

Those who are baptized are united to Christ in a death like his; buried with him in death, they are given life again with him, and with him they rise again. For Baptism recalls and makes present the paschal mystery itself because in Baptism we pass from the death of sin into life. ("General Introduction," *Christian Initiation,* #6)

Your ways, O Lord, are love and truth, to those who keep your covenant. (Psalm 25:10, As given for the Rite of Election, *RCIA,* prior to #118)

The catechumens should be properly initiated into the mystery of salvation.... (*Catechism of the Catholic Church,* #1248).

Special Questions

This section will address some of the specific issues and questions that have not yet been addressed in this booklet. If you have a question that has not been addressed, please contact your RCIA coordinator or your pastor.

■ **My husband wants to become Catholic. Can I be his sponsor?**

Although in some circumstances a spouse may be a fine choice, many RCIA coordinators believe that someone other than the Catholic spouse makes a more effective sponsor. The supportive spouse already has an important role in the candidate's journey of faith. No one can duplicate or replace the special partnership that the spouse has with the candidate. The spouse has a unique and prominent role in supporting, encouraging, sharing faith, answering questions, praying with and for the candidate. Thus, even though the spouse may want to be the sponsor, many coordinators and RCIA leadership teams find it helpful to have someone else be the parish sponsor.

The Catholic spouse is already a kind of sponsor given the very nature of the marriage relationship. A parish sponsor other than the spouse is able to bring a different perspective to the Catholic Christian way of life. The candidate may (or may not) already know a spouse's view on various issues. A parish sponsor may be able to discuss topics and concerns in a way that is different from the spouse. It's good to broaden the candidate's view.

Also, the candidate and the spouse may be new to the parish. Having someone other than a spouse affords the inquirer an opportunity to meet others in the parish and make new friendships. It's hard for a spouse to acquaint the candidate to a parish if they are both new to a particular community.

Moreover, every person's situation is unique. In some cases Catholic spouses want to be very involved. And, the candidate wants them involved. In other cases, it's best for the candidate to have some independence and feel freedom to make a decision about Catholicism on her or his own. In many situations, it's helpful for spouses to come to RCIA sessions even if they are not serving as sponsors. And, spouses who are not Roman Catholic are certainly encouraged to be active and involved in the process as well. In any case, the RCIA coordinator and the candidate decide together what is best.

■ **My family and I have been asked to sponsor a woman and her children. The mother is a baptized Lutheran and the children are unbaptized. What do we need to know about sponsoring a family?**

In this case, the woman and her children need sponsors. Although the parent is the children's primary "sponsor" in the broad sense, the children need parish sponsors as much as the mother does.

Regarding parish sponsors, everything that has been said about being a sponsor for adults applies to being a sponsor for children. Of course, what has been said must be adapted in a developmentally appropriate way. Children who are older than seven years go through the RCIA the same as adults. That is, the children go through the same periods and steps that adults do. They, too, go on a journey of conversion. Thus, they need someone to walk with them on the journey.

Therefore, in this scenario, a sponsor would sponsor the entire family: the woman and her children. Here, the sponsor is actually a sponsoring family. Thus, the entire sponsoring family helps, supports, encourages and guides the initiation family. The sponsoring family would also stand up with the initiation family at the Rite of Acceptance Into the Order of Catechumens.

An ideal situation would be that the sponsoring family has children of similar ages to the initiation family. In this way, the children help to "sponsor" the children. Children introduce children to the Catholic Christian way of life. Sponsoring children serve as companions to the initiation children.

Therefore, the roles and responsibilities of being a sponsoring family are the same as being an individual sponsor. The qualities of a sponsor are the same. The suggestions for what to do with your candidate are somewhat the same, though the activities would be more family- and child-oriented.

If you are a parent with children, you already know what is appropriate, helpful and realistic for a family. Talk honestly about how you pass on faith to your children. Talk about the informal ways you teach children to pray, such as bedtime prayers and mealtime prayers. Use your own good family sense when supporting and guiding an initiation family. Just be you.

■ I still don't feel comfortable in my relationship with my candidate. I've tried, but the relationship just isn't working. What should I do?

Sometimes two people just "click"—and sometimes they don't. First of all, do not worry. Sometimes sponsor-candidate relationships do not work. When two strangers are paired together, there is always the chance that the relationship won't work. Sometimes there is a specific obstacle, but mostly it's an intangible difference in personalities. Try not to be discouraged. It is no one's fault. Your efforts are appreciated and you may be paired with someone later. Go and talk to your RCIA or sponsor coordinator right away. Don't let it go on for too long. You'll probably both be happier if you make a change.

■ Do I need training to be a sponsor?

Yes! If sponsor training is not available in your parish, ask your parish RCIA coordinator if training can be offered. Some of the topics to be included in sponsor training are:

- An overview of the RCIA.
- What is conversion in initiation?
- Being a companion.
- How to be a witness.
- How to be an active listener.
- The sponsor's role in the rites of the RCIA.
- The specific responsibilities at our parish.

If your RCIA coordinator is not able to offer training sessions, ask your coordinator if you could gather with a few other sponsors for some discussion on the topics listed above. These topics are briefly covered in this book. Use the discussion questions to give you advice on how to be a good sponsor. And have a neophyte come and talk with you about what candidates are looking for in sponsors.

Conclusion

Because of who you are and the qualities you have, you have been called and chosen for this important ministry. Take it seriously, but not too seriously. Enjoy the journey! Be open, honest and be yourself. We think you'll find that your own conversion is deepened, and that your faith is enriched and renewed by sharing it with another. May you rediscover Jesus Christ as you travel along the way.